KAVALA

PHILIPPI

The Azure Town

EDITIONS
TOUBI'S

© Copyright   MICHAEL TOUBIS PUBLICATIONS S.A.
                 Nisiza Karela, Koropi, Attiki.
                 Telephone: +30 210 6029974, Fax: +30 210 6646856
                 Web Site: http://www.toubis.gr

ISBN: 960-540-280-7

CONTENTS

CONTENTS

KAVALA

Kavala, the azure town, the most beautiful port of the Aegean. No other place quite like it exists. An impressive combination of sea and mountain which fascinates all visitors on first sight.

Kavala is built amphitheatrically on the slopes of Mt. Symbolon and is surrounded by verdant forest. She has the most beautiful beaches and the bluest sea at her feet, whilst the old aqueduct, the castle, the paved alleyways of Panagia and its imperious neoclassical buildings are miraculous witnesses to the history of the town. Kavala's natural beauty has often been the topic of song, and great are the number who have admired her since antiquity. She offers the peace and carelessness of a small provincial resort whilst, at the same time, displaying elements of splendid gaiety in a cosmopolitan atmosphere of which many traditional holiday resorts would be jealous. However, it is not only the town which enthrals but the entire prefecture which surrounds Kavala. Monuments and sights combine to create the impression that, in Kavala, time passes slower than anywhere else.

The stunning azure of the sky and sea of Kavala make her worthy to claim her title. At night, impressive reds and oranges add a different tone to the uniqueness of the landscape.

The Azure Town

Nature and Location

The prefecture of Kavala belongs to eastern Macedonia and is located between the Nestos river to the east and the Strymon river to the west, which also form the natural boundaries of the prefecture. It has an area of 2,109 square kilometres and borders on to the prefecture of Xanthi to the east, the prefecture of Drama to the north, and that of Serres to the west, whilst to the south it is washed by the stunningly blue Aegean. The island of Thassos also belongs to the prefecture of Kavala, as do the uninhabited islets of Thassopoula and Fidonissi. The soil of the area is rich and fertile, especially in the plains to the east and west of the town.

In the western corner of the prefecture, looms the Pangaion mountain whose highest summit reaches 1,956 metres, whilst in the northeast lies the mountainous chain of Lekani. Finally, the mountain of Ypsarion rises on Thassos to a height of 1,160 metres.

As far as the subsoil is concerned, a number of hydrocarbon deposits have been discovered in the sea between Kavala and Thassos, and there is hope that similar deposits will also be found on both banks of the Nestos river. Systematic research has been carried out in this area since 1972. There are also peat deposits in the Philippi marshes which have been drained by a large purpose-built ditch. The subsoil is rich in iron ore which can be found in a number of areas within the mainland prefecture and, primarily, on Thassos. Research also continues for the purpose of locating exploitable gold deposits on the Pangaion mountain and along the Nestos river. Deposits of uranium in the area are considered important, and there has also been systematic exploitation of the schist in the area of Pangaion in recent years. The climate of the prefecture is mild; Mediterranean on the coast but becoming increasingly continental as one proceeds north, being characteristically cold in winter and warm in the summer. The fertile soil of the area is ideal for cultivation, especially of asparagus, grapes, cotton, olives and tobacco. The population of Kavala numbers 145,000 inhabitants; people who, in addition to their agriculture, of the prefecture are involved in fishing and trading. In recent years, however, the growth and development of tourism has steered the locals towards professions with a direct connection to the tourist industry.

═══	Asphalt road
────	Non asphalt road
═══	Minor road
⊢16⊣	Distance in km
🏛	Archaeological site
🏛	Monastery
🏰	Castle

Mother Nature has been very generous to the region of Kavala and has given her the most beautiful beaches. Most notable are the bays of Eleftheraion, Nea Iraklitsa and Keramoti with the marvellous coastline catering to the visitor who can relish in the cool waters and explore the magical seabed.

The regions of the Nestos and Pangaion are endowed with the richest flora and fauna. The area of the delta of the Nestos river is particularly special and is one of the eleven national wetland areas of international importance. In this sanctuary, hospitality is extended to otters, jackals, wild cats and wolves, and 310 species of birds have been spotted, among them, eagles, gulls and herons. In the narrows of the Nestos river, semi-wild horses, rare species of predatory birds, reptiles and insects all find refuge. It is a place where they can feel safe from any danger.

The rich seabed, the crystal clear springs and the shady valleys favour the development of the rich and unique fauna of the area.

As far as the flora are concerned, one can find something really quite unique. There are flowers, plants and wild trees which cannot be found anywhere else and many scientists come here to study and admire them.

There are many lakes in the region of Chryssoupolis, the largest of which is the large lake of Alaca Göl, where the vegetation is very rich and the dominant species is water lily. Finally, the Pangaion mountain is covered in immense fir trees and plane trees with some areas remaining trackless due to the sheer abundance of the vegetation.

Mother Nature offers generous gifts to Kavala. Her verdant mountains and picturesque lakes abound with wild vegetation.

HISTORY

Ancient - Byzantine and more Recent Times

Neapolis, Christoupolis and Kavala; three names for the same town which reflect three different periods of history -the ancient Greek, the Byzantine and the more recent. Before the Archaic age, the ancient site of the town does not appear to have been inhabited. However, the existence of a small Neolithic settlement has been discovered on the eastern side of the town. This settlement, along with the scant remains of the wall of the Antissara in the area of Kipoupolis, are, however, not strong enough evidence from which one could conclude the existence of prehistoric settlements. According to the archaeologist Dimitris Lazaridis, the explanation is simple: the prehistoric inhabitants of the area were not involved with the sea but with the land. They did not, therefore, settle down close to the sea but further inland of Kavala during the Neolithic and Bronze Age.

Neapolis, which was a colony of Thassos, was built on the peninsula where today one finds Panagia. This site was of immense strategic and commercial importance because of the road which passes through here connecting Thrace to Macedonia.

The silver stater from Neapolis depicting the head of a Gorgon.

Ancient Times

A date for the founding of ancient Kavala cannot be discerned from the historical sources. However, more recent research has indicated that, in the middle of the 7th century BC along with the new emigrants from Paros, the inhabitants of Thassos established the town of Neapolis, present-day Kavala, in an attempt to confront invasions from Thrace. Ancient Neapolis, because of her privileged geographical location, was an important port. It was the doorway to the rich area of Datos and the gold-bearing Pangaion mountain and, naturally, it was the route connecting east with west. It was via this route that the Persians travelled during their expedition against Greece, as did the Macedonian kings Philip II and Alexander the Great on their way to subjugate the Greek towns in Thrace. Life in Neapolis began around 650 - 625 BC and their first focus of worship in the town was the patron goddess Parthenos. Evidence of the town's autonomy comes from the silver mint which begins a little before 500 BC. The first coins, the so-called staters, depict mainly the hideous head of a Gorgon and on the other side an impressed square.

Terracotta black-figured amphora, beginning of the 5th century BC. From the cemetery of ancient Oisyme.

Neapolis became a member of the Athenian Alliance after the battle of Plataea and the departure of the Persians. Neapolis was also the first town mentioned in the Athenain tax-lists of 454/453 BC, with a fixed contribution to the Alliance fund of 1,000 drachmas a year. The Alliance, along with the amiable relationship between Neapolis and Athens, continued even during the period of conflict between the Athenians and the Thassiots and also during the final period of the Peloponnesian War.

In the year 346 BC, Thrace was ruled by Philip who, in 340 BC, also conquered Thassos. The silver mint of Neapolis ceased at this point, the town lost it's autonomy and became the sea port of the Macedonian town of Philippi. From then on, the name of Neapolis is mentioned only incidentally as, for instance, in a resolution from Philippi in 243/41 BC which was found on Kos and in which it is mentioned that at the port of Neapolis, the theoroi embarked and disembarked during their announcement of the celebration of the Asclepians.

Roman Period

In 189 BC, the supreme commander Manlius Vulso, returning from his expedition against Antiochus of Syria, passed through Neapolis. In 42 BC, the Republican leaders Brutus and Cassius used her as a base for their fleet during the dramatic battle of Philippi which had historic results that determined the fate of the Roman Empire. After the foundation of the Roman colony at Philippi, it is certain that eminent Romans from this colony settled down in beautiful Neapolis. Also coming from this time are the sarcophagi with Latin inscriptions which were found in Kavala some centuries ago and which are now in the museum of the town.

Byzantine Period

Perhaps around the beginning of the 8th or 9th centuries AD, the name of the town changes from Neapolis and becomes Christoupolis. When the issues of the Byzantine State began to be organized, Christoupolis belonged to the theme of Strymon, which included the area of Strymon as far as the Nestos river. In the 9th and 14th centuries, when the Slavs invaded the area, Christoupolis always remained as the last stronghold in the area; a barrier to the invaders and the only port providing communication with Thessaloniki. In AD 926, the general of the theme of Strymon, King Kladon, rebuilt the walls of the town. In 1097, the troops of the first Crusade passed Christoupolis, and in 1193, after the abolition of the Byzantine State by the Franks, the town fell into the hands of the Lombards who began to make renovations. However, in 1208, after an attempt to invade and plunder Philippi, the Lombards were defeated by the Franks and all those who were not arrested only survived by running away.

Corinthian alabastron, end of the 7th to beginning of the 6th century BC. From the cemetery of ancient Oisyme. Kavala Archaeological Museum.

Roman sarcophagus from the Archaeological Museum of Kavala.

In the 14th century, Christoupolis again had a major role to play in history. The Serbs and Turks claimed eastern Macedonia whilst, at the same time, the Byzantine State experienced a deathblow due to internal complications.

In 1321 - 1328, during the first period of dispute, the name of Christoupolis became foremost of all. In April 1346, Kral Dusan was crowned king and emperor of the Serbs and Romans and gained control of the region of eastern Macedonia, whilst Christoupolis belonged to the Byzantines as one of the last props of the State. In 1375, the region of eastern Macedonia came under the command of the Greeks.

Turkish Occupation

The Turks, who came across the area of eastern Macedonia at the beginning of the 14th century and plundered it every now and then, conquered Christoupolis in 1387. For the next four years, until 1391, they occupied and destroyed her.

In 1425, the castle of Christoupolis suffered attacks by the Venetians who finally managed to conquer her. Their occupation, however, lasted less than a month as the Turks returned and, after a siege of twenty days, reconquered her. At some point around then, the history of Christoupolis stops and around the end of the 15th and beginning of the 16th centuries, Christoupolis, changes name and is from then on mentioned as Kavala. For a short while, this new name was used accompanied by the old to avoid confusion.

Around 1526, the new settlers were Turks and Greeks, who may have come from the surrounding areas, along with a number of Jewish prisoners whom the Turks brought with them after the war in Hungary of the same year.

The surrounding walls gave security to the new inhabitants, but their numbers grew to such heights that the old fortres of Panagia was unable to meet the needs of this new, re-emerging town.

Around 1530, large projects were begun in Kavala which would change the view of the landscape and of the new town; projects which would help improve living conditions. Then, under the command of Suleiman II the Magnificent, the town expanded to the port and a new wall was built.

In addition to this, on the site of the old wall, one of the most impressive monuments of Kavala was raised -the aqueduct known as Kamares. In April 1611, five galleys of the Duke of Florence arrived in the port of Kavala. They disembarked and attempted to occupy the fortress, but did not succeed and the pirates eventually gave up and left.

In the 17th century, there was intense rebellion from the crews of the beys' galleys who were bent on freedom. In particular, in 1603 the slaves of Ahmet bey of Kavala rebelled and took him, along with his galley, to Italy where they killed him.

In 1619, the Christian oarsmen of the galley of then bey of Kavala also rebelled and left with the ship. Pirate invasions against Thassos and Kavala also continued in the second half of the 17th century, but without serious consequences. At the beginning of the 18th century, the port of Kavala and its importance in trade, increased more and more. Kavala was used as a storage depot for merchandise from Smyrna and Egypt, as well as for products from Thassos and the rest of the Aegean islands. At this point cannon balls also constituted freight, being produced in Eleftheroupolis and sent to their destination of Constantinople.

The development of the town and the port continued in the 19th century. The Greek element expanded and the Greeks played an important role in the economy and trade of the area. In this period, many travellers and scientists visited Kavala and, from about the middle of the same century, they set about the task of creating and organizing a better way of life.

For many years the old church of Panagia, which is located at the end of the peninsula, was the centre of Christianity.

View of Kavala in the 1920s.

At the end of the 19th century the Greek community of Kavala was stronger than ever. The Greek population reached 10,000 whilst trade, shipping and the arts were in Greek hands, and a large number of cottage industries were flourishing. Schools, hospitals, public buildings and a sports centre were built.

Festivities in the port.
The crowd accompanies their king.

Liberation - More Recent Times

The 20th century finds Kavala in her golden era. From 1903 to 1909, the Greek population, with a strong sense of national pride, participate in the Macedonian War and also help in the defence against the Bulgarian propaganda of the guerrillas.

In October 1912, the Bulgarian guerrillas occupy Kavala without any resistance from the Turks. A time of oppression, torment and captivity follows, but the message of freedom is brought by Greek ships.

An armada, with its flagship the illustrious battleship Averoff and using Thassos as its base, patrols the waters off Kavala. On the 25th of June 1913, Greek ships appear and on the morning of the following day, the 26th of June, the destroyer Doxa sails into the bay of Kavala and occupies the town.

On the 27th of June 1913, Admiral Kountouriotis and his staff, disembark in the midst of a festive atmosphere in Kavala. He goes first to the Government House and then to the church where he appears at the doxology chanted for the liberation of the town. On the same afternoon, he sends from the warship, Averoff, an unforgettable radiogram :

"From Averoff on the 27th of June. Time, 5 and 30 pm. Today, the occupation of Kavala is officially proclaimed.

We cleaned the surrounding areas of guerrillas and any stray, capable Bulgarian soldiers. Passions are soaring. The Turks co-operated fully. KOUNTOURIOTIS"

In 1922, with the catastrophe in Asia Minor and the exchange of population, about 25,000 refugees settled in Kavala.

Up until 1930, the economic boom of Kavala had reached its peak and the town became the largest centre for the processing of tobacco in the wider area of eastern Macedonia and Thrace. Large foreign tobacco-trading companies settled down in the town and the traffic in her port doubled.

The flourishing of the tobacco trade and the growth of the population resulted in the creation of a large working class - the tobacco workers were calculated to number some 20,000 in 1928- who organized themselves into strong unions and fought vigorously for their rights.

The social aspect of the town altered and the mobilizations of the workers became more frequent. Difficult years followed; the dictatorship of Metaxas, the Second World War and the Civil War. The tobacco trade dwindled, unemployment drove the masses to emigration, the population shrank and Kavala lost, possibly forever, her pre-war glory. Only during the last few decades , with the establishment of the fertilizer factory in Nea Karvali, and the discovery of oil deposits at Prinos, has an important development been reintroduced which, together with its advantages, brings with it also all the disadvantages of a modern industrial civilization.

CAVALLA (NÉAP

Kavala (Neapolis), view from the sea. Lithogr

Hanhart, lit

) FROM THE SEA .

ublication of the Holy Metropolis of Philippi.

3 CULTURE &

Kavala is a gifted place as far as its nature and people are concerned. The idyllic landscape in which Kavala is built, as well as the 'mixture' of many different races (Pontians, people from Asia Minor, Thracians, Sarakatsani, make her especially interesting as far as the cultural life and her traditions are concerned.

The cultural events reflect the long centuries of faithful adherence to the manners and customs which the inhabitants have managed to keep alive through the ages. Also, in regards to the arts and letters, Kavala has given birth to people of spirit who have achieved marvellous things inspired by the beauties of the town.

Despite the difficulties to which they have been subjected, the inhabitants of the prefecture have managed to form a cheerful temperament. They are merry and optimistic but also a people with kindness and love who will welcome you from the first moment they meet you. These people are the ones who spread to the new generation the need for artistic and spiritual creation inspired by the traditions which are the quintessence of the wisdom of decades.

The people of Kavala are ardent merry-makers which is proven by the dances and the festivals they organize. The celebration on the day of a saint, or of a happy event, gives the opportunity to organize such a festival and event the spectators are carries away by the dancing.

TRADITION

Manners and Customs

The important celebrations of Orthodoxy are accompanied by a series of traditional customs.

On New Years Eve, after the cutting of the pitta and after the house has been infused with the incense on the table, the girl of the house begins her attempt to find out how her luck will turn out. Three small balls of thread -one white, one red and the third blue- are placed under her pillow, together with the first piece of the pitta. The next morning, when the girl awakes, she takes all three balls of thread and throws them high in front of her. If the first to hit the ground is the blue one, the year will be poor as far as marriage and happiness are concerned.

For New Years Day, there is also the custom of breaking a rose on the landing so that the year will go well. Another custom, involves a small, innocent child stepping into the house in order to bring luck to the house and so that the coming year will be happy and rich, with no hostilities or arguments.

At Easter, except for the traditional breaking of the eggs, on the night of the Resurrection, when the family comes back from church, there is the custom that the father makes a cross on the front door frame with the smoke from the candle burning with the Holy Light.

One of the charming traditions of the area is that which is performed during weddings in the village of Domatia. On the day of the wedding, all the young spinsters gather in the bride's room and help the bride to dress whilst, at the same time, a woman sings songs about the bride, having been informed of her task only the day before.

When the dressing is finished, they fill a large copper pan with rice and the bride steps into it wearing her wedding shoe. Before she steps into the pan, however, the young women write their names on the sole of the shoe and whoever's name comes off will be married first and soon.

A labarum from a Sarakatsanian wedding.

Also, before the dressing of the bride is begun, her mother breaks a pitta over her head. All the girls break off a piece of this pitta (without cutting it with a knife) and put it, the following night, underneath their pillows in order to dream of the one they will marry. The pitta is made without yeast but has many spices. On Thassos, there is an even more enjoyable custom which involves the best man riding a donkey on his way to collect the bride. All the friends of the bride are with her in the same room she was being dressed, and they ask the best man for money to give her. The bazaar that follows between the best man and the friends of the bride is a real feast.

On the groom's side also, all his friends gather at his house and shave him in a traditional way whilst, at the same time, 'teasing' him incessantly. Similar customs abound in the area and have their roots in Thrace, Asia Minor, Pontos, Thassos and other regions. Some of them are kept faithfully whilst others have been all but forgotten.

The eve of the celebration of Agios Theodoros is devoted solely to the young men. The customs that exist on this day concern the dreams and desires of the young men. They originated in Thrace but continue to survive up to today in this region, especially in the area of Chryssoupolis.

As soon as the sun begins to set, the young men gather together and hold a meeting. Their aim is to steal an object or a tool from the yards of the houses where an unwed girl lives. The stolen items are placed in central parts of the town or village and the owners go down the next day to retrieve them.

By doing this, the young men attempt to show their interest in the young women. On the same day, the young women have their own customs. They must bake an armyrokoulouro (salted bread ring), but the flour and the salt that are needed must be obtained from three different houses.

They then make the dough and bake the bread ring in a house that is far away. After the baking, the bread is shared among an odd number of girls -three or five. Finally, in the evening before they go to bed, each girl eats her piece and repeats the following lines three times:

Agios Theodoros the Great and Wonder Worker,
you travel 'round the mountains
and destiny encounter.
If you find mine too, be it foul or fair,
bring it, tonight, to be with me here.

When they finish reading, they drink a sip of water and go to bed. The man who brings them water in their dreams will be the one they will marry.

Also, one day before the day of Agios Theodoros, the young women place a sieve on top of a red cloth. They take barley seeds and throw them into the sieve, saying:

Barley seed, up grows wheat,
my love will come too and together we'll reap.

Cultural Events

In the town of Kavala, as well as in the surrounding areas, the cultural and folklore events are an important part of the life of the people. They are events organized with much enthusiasm and are anticipated with great suspense. There are twenty seven cultural societies in Kavala which organize a significant number of activities. Quite a few participate in cultural events in foreign countries and have won prizes. Some, Lyceum Hellenides for example the are the oldest and most important societies around. Very often balls and dancing events are organized by the associations in beautiful sections of the town. The municipal theatre of Kavala is also one of the vehicles which arranges the most important cultural events in Kavala. The foremost and most famous of these is the **Philippi-Thassos Festival** which began in 1957 with 'Electra', a work by Euripides, performed by the Kostis Livaditis Society of Ancient Tragedy. The performance was put on in the ancient theatre of Philippi which had to be partially rebuilt in order for the festival to continue to be held there. The authorities, along with a number of eminent and anonymous people of Kavala, lent their support so that the repairs could be carried out. The establishment of the State Theatre of Northern Greece in 1961, gave new impetus to the festival when, in the summer, the headquarters of the theatre was once again transferred to the ancient theatre of Philippi and Kavala, whilst performances are also held in the ancient theatre of Thassos. Today this is the largest festival in Northern Greece thanks to the contributions but also to the promotions by the municipality of Kavala. It has become the centre of cultural, social and civil life and creation for the whole region.

The programme of the Philippi-Thassos Festival begins, usually, at the beginning of March each year, when the ancient drama productions by the largest theatrical companies of the country are announced.

In addition to the ancient drama, however, there are also other types of art shown during the festival, such as music and dancing. It is a fact that the most famous artists from Greece and abroad have come to the Philippi-Thassos Festival due to the many premieres which have been performed there.

The feast of 'ELEFTHERION' ('FREEDOM') in Kavala is one of the more important cultural events by the municipal theatre.

It is organized every year from the 25th of June to the 5th of July and is devoted to the liberation of Kavala (which was achieved on the 26th of June 1913), but also to the celebration of the patron saint of the town, the Apostle Paul, on the 29th of June.

Within this feast, events are hosted which show the work of all creators of Kavala in every aspect of cultural creation and artistic activity, such as dancing troupes, theatrical companies of cultural societies, athletic societies, societies of painters and many others.

The events take place in the wonderful fortress of the town and in other places throughout Kavala which have been chosen as suitable, such as the small wood of Panagouda, the area of the lighthouse, the small theatre behind the statue of Mehmet-Ali in Panagia, and the square of Kapnergati. Finally, the municipality sponsors the organization of the evening of the Kavalian Emigrants on the first Monday in August, to which feast all Kavalians from abroad are invited. Dancing troupes and orchestras from Kavala take part. Another important event is the folk festival of Chryssoupolis which takes place at the beginning of September and during which small exhibitions are held and dance troupes, from the area and from outside, perform. Concerts and other musical events are also organized

Cultural events take first priority among the artistic activities of Kavala.

Equally famous is the Carnival of Thassos which attracts large numbers of visitors from all over Greece. Having it's roots in the feasts of Dionysus, the carnival is an event which is celebrated in almost every village on the island. People in costumes, lewd songs and verses, as well as free food and wine are predominant on these days.

The folklore events of Xanthi are also well known and are the second largest in the country after those at Patra. It is a fact, however, that in recent years Xanthi appears to have outpaced Patra. Attendance numbers during the 'Feast of the Potatoes' in Lekani are considerable as they are for the revived custom of the Sarakatsanian wedding on Mount Pangaion.

We should not forget to mention the very important pan-Hellenic cultural event which takes place every autumn close to Drama - the International Festival of Short Drama Films.

Finally, the international folklore festival 'Ilios kai Petra' ('Sun and Stone'), which is organized by the N. Karvalis Centre for Tradition and Culture, is an event attended by countries from all over the world.
The events of the festival are held in the small, open-air N. Karvalis theatre, but to facilitate the better running of the festival and cater to a more comfortable residence for visiting groups, a large 'folklore village' will soon be ready.

Arts and Letters

Since 1950, the spiritual activities in Kavala have been developing significantly. Many are the men of letters and poets who were born in Kavala and have important works to show.

The international folklore festival of "Ilios kai Petra" ("Sun and Stone").

Vassilis Vassilikos is the most famous of the Greek writers still alive. He was born in Kavala in 1934 where he spent his childhood years. He is one of the most charismatic figures of modern Greek prose and many of his works have been translated into a number of different languages. His first book was the novel 'The Story of Jason'. To his most famous and beloved works belong the multi-part story "The Last Goodbye' and the, perhaps better, work «The Flame of Love'.

In poetry, **Prodromos Markoglou** is one of the most important figures from the area. He was born in Kavala in 1935, studied economics in Athens, and has been living in Thessaloniki since 1971. In addition to his important poetic anthologies: 'The Confined', 'Survey' and "The Waves and the Voices', he has also written prose. His poems have been published in many magazines and newspapers and have been translated into English, Italian, Polish and Rumanian.

A third important literary figure from Kavala is **Chronis Missios** who was born here in 1930. His parents were tobacco workers and he himself worked as a vendor in the port with a small trunk and left school during the second year of primary school. He was left with very strong convictions, was imprisoned by the junta and was almost executed. He gained amnesty in 1973, however, and since then lives as a free man in Athens. His first book was entitled 'You Were Killed Early', and many more, very successful, works followed.

Diamantis Axiotis, born in Kavala in 1942 where he still lives, is another well known writer. He has been a member of the Society of Greek Writers since 1988 and a founding member of the Society of Writers of Macedonia-Thrace from 1992. His poetic anthologies 'Ichor', 'Percentage of Liability' and others are famous. Other collections by him: 'Poets from Kavala' and 'Short Stories from Photis Prassinis', are important works as is his prose work of the collection of short stories 'Half of the Centaurs'.

In 1912, in Madyto of eastern Thrace, another notable literary figure of Kavala was born; **Photis Prassinis**. He came to Kavala in 1923 as a refugee when he was eleven years old and, being fatherless, had to struggle to survive from a young age. In 1944 he published his first short story in the Magazine "Macedonian Letters' of Thessaloniki. He wrote about thirty one short stories and presented a complete series of 'Travelling' texts which are descriptions and impressions from his trips to Thassos, Nestos and Edessa. He died in 1973.

Kosmas Charpantidis is one of the youngest literary notables of Kavala. Born in 1959 close to the Greek/Bulgarian border, he has lived, as a lawyer, in Kavala since 1964. In 1993 he published the short stories Mania of the Town' which presents a personal view of the town of Kavala. Other important works followed.

These spiritual creators, and others perhaps less well known, spread the name of Kavala throughout and without the borders of Greece.

In addition to the literary arts, the plastic arts of Kavala are especially well developed. Sculptors, hagiographers and painters have all shown, and continue to show, important works which present the town, not only to Greece, but also abroad. Some of these artists display their creations in their own workshops but they also make use of the various art exhibitions.

As far as sculpture is concerned, a distinguished figure can be found in **Dimosthenis Sotiroudis**. Born in 1941, he studied sculpture at the Free School of Fine Arts and afterwards at the State Academy of Fine Arts in Stuttgart, Germany. He travelled to America and finally settled down in Kavala. He is a very important sculptor and has a rich collection to show. He has held sixteen personal exhibitions in Greece as well as abroad and his work has been awarded positive criticism from prominent art historians.

Also notable is the hagiographic work of **Themis Simitsakos** which includes portable icons and memorial groups which are deeply influenced by Byzantine art. He was born in 1959 in Canada where he studied fine arts and was initiated into Byzantine painting at the hagiographical home of the Daniilaion on Mount Athos. His work can be found in private collections and in the churches of the Holy Cathedral of Philippi, Neapolis and Thassos, and he has participated in a number of exhibitions. Additionally notable is the hagiographical work of **Babis Gamvrelis**, also influenced by Byzantine art. Born in 1958 in Kavala, he learned from being in close proximity to his father who worked on Mount Athos for three years. Gamvrelis has been professionally involved in hagiography for twenty years. His work includes portable icons which can be found in private collections and in churches throughout Greece and abroad.

Finally, in the discipline of painting, **Themis Kelekis** is a distinguished individual. Born in 1936 in Kavala he was taught by the notable painter G Chatzopoulos, his uncle on his mother's side, and completed his studies in Paris. He managed to gain international recognition for his unique and pioneering techniques, as well as receiving eight important artistic prizes. He paints without imitating any other artist or style, completing his works with a palette knife. He has successfully participated in a large number of exhibitions, and lives and works in Kavala.

Theatre

The founding, in July 1993, of the Municipal Regional Theatre of Kavala is also included within the framework of spiritual obsession.

Events at the municipal music school of Kavala.

Since January 1994, a significant attempt is being undertaken to upgrade the cultural life of the town. The opening of the theatre has been embraced by the people and it has proved only the beginning of substantial works.

The theatre of Kavala does not confine its plays only to the town but also stages them in the neighbouring prefectures of Drama, Xanthi, Komotini, and Serres as well as Kozani, Veria and the Theatre Royal in Thessaloniki and Athens. Some of the plays which have been put on by the theatrical group of Kavala are: 'The Road Passes From Within' by Iakovos Kambanelis, Black Comedy', 'The Cunning of Skapen" and ('The Island of the Slaves').

Today, with generations of young artists in the actors' as well as musicians' roles, the theatre tries to raise its levels even higher and conquer new heights.

Music

Together with the Municipal Regional tTheatre of Kavala, the municipal music school also contributes to the spiritual uplift of the area. The music school is the oldest one in town, having been founded in 1939 as an element of the municipality of Kavala with the aim of spreading the love of music to the younger generation, and of maintaining the town band. In 1983, the music school opened its doors to all the children of the town by organizing lessons in which the children could learn instruments which were not, until then, taught in the town.

The result was quite impressive: 600 - 700 students now study in the school and 40 music teachers run classes in stringed instruments, wind instruments, percussion instruments, piano, guitar, accordion, monodies of higher theories and introduction to music.

The musical school has, since 1890, been hosted in a privately-owned neoclassical building which was donated and restored by the municipality of Kavala.

In addition to the classrooms, the building

The neoclassical building which hosts the oldest music education establishment of the town, the municipal music school.

has a library, and a substantial concert hall which holds cultural events by the school and other cultural associations of Kavala. Many students have completed the full cycle of study at the school and obtained their certificates and diplomas, whilst the most gifted have been awarded prizes in various pan-Hellenic musical competitions, and some follow brilliant carriers abroad.

During it's participation in the cultural events of the town, the music school organizes concerts, inviting musicians of international renown together with the Camerata Orchestra of Athens to give educational programmes.

The school itself has three orchestras; the 'Akordeonata', the only orchestra of accordions in Kavala; the big band 'The Other Side', a jazz orchestra and the 'Symphonietta', a small symphonic orchestra of stringed instruments.

Architecture

Until the middle of the 19th century, Kavala was restricted to the area of Panagia. The houses of traditional construction and art are examples of an old forgotten time. With the expansion of Kavala beyond the limits of Panagia, the Turks, Jews, Armenians and western Europeans began to build houses and gave a look to the new town which was composed of completely different architectural styles to those used in the houses of Panagia. All styles were used and gradually appeared either in the western European or the Greek quarters. Not even German baroque was missing nor German rococo, nor the French rococo of Beau Art.

The first houses of the new town were those that were built in the Agios Ioannis quarter by the Greeks. They have elements of traditional architecture combined with neoclassical elements of the time. The most representative building of these times is the main Town Hall.

The two decades either side of 1900 were the most productive period of the flourishing tobacco trade in Kavala.
At this time the large warehouses for the storage of tobacco were built along with many important mansions. By then the traditional architecture was abandoned and the neoclassicism became dominant.

Characteristics of the architecture of that period are the fake columns and capitals, the architraves, the small pediments, the enclosed gardens, the marble stairs, the terracotta balusters, the wide verandas and the statuettes with ancient Greek themes.

During the first decade of the 20th century, the houses belonging to the Greeks, Jews and Turks were built.
The architectural elements used in these are a vivid reminder of Anatolia and have a certain exotic element about them.
In about the ten years that followed 1924, Kavala expanded and the only consideration was to provide accommodation for the people coming in to the town, predominantly from the catastrophe in Asia Minor. A number of settlements were thus created, including Pentakossia, Chilia and the refugee settlement of Agia Varvara, all with almost identical houses built by the same people and paid for by the state.

Up to 1950, and possibly until 1960, Kavala managed to hold on to her old colour. Nowadays, however, she has become just another concrete town and there are only a few houses left to remind us of the old days.

The attempt at restoration of the buildings and preservation of the traditional architecture, have allowed the town to regain some of her old colour.

People and Occupations

The people of the area of Kavala have been involved for a long time in trade, fishing and agriculture. As well as her important position, her large port gave her the opportunity to develop these three activities perfectly.

Trade is one of the most important activities of the inhabitants, because there are many trading outlets; representatives of companies that serve all of eastern Macedonia and Thrace, as well as cottage and larger industries.

Many of these larger industries manufacture products which are distributed, not only to the whole of Greece, but even exported. In these businesses, a major percentage of the working population is employed.

Kavala was once the Mecca of tobacco and there were many warehouse and shops, but the time when Kavala was full of tobacco workers now belongs to the past.

Another prime profession for the locals is fishing. The natural richness of Kavala and the sea have, for years, supported those who carry out their jobs in the traditional way. A large number of trawlers and larger vessels leave each day to make their catch, and a real feast is held every morning at the famous wharf of the town where one can find the largest and freshest fish on sale.

The fertile soil and rich waters of Kavala are very good for agriculture and fishing.

Agriculture, too, is one of the old and well established professions of the inhabitants. The soil around Kavala is very fertile and ideal for the cultivation of a wide range of produce.

In recent years, the farmers have begun to systematize their work and improve the cultivation process, a fact which has resulted in high quality goods which are known even outside Greece, such as asparagus, grapes, kiwis, olive oil and olives, soya, wheat and many others.

Unions have also been formed which assist the producers in obtaining fertilizer and seeds at a reduced rate and also helps them turn over their produce to foreign markets.

We should not forget to mention here, the vineyards in the area of Peramos and Eleftheron from which come first class wine.

Social progress and technological development became the reasons why many of the traditional professions, which are remarkable even today, began to disappear: the wandering professionals who travelled around the area on foot, selling products and offering unique services such as chair repairman or dove-cote mender.

Today there still exist some street vendors, such as the ice-cream seller, the corn seller, the antique trader and the cobbler, but the old professions have lost their former glory and are gradually being abandoned.

*Views of a traditional way of life
that is slowly disappearing.*

Archaeological Museum

In 1934, the history of the museum of Kavala began along with the establishment of the archaeological service, the first curator of antiquities being Mr. G. Bakalakis.

Before his replacement, the antiquities of eastern Macedonia and Thrace where housed in the antiquities unit of Macedonia which had its headquarters in Thessaloniki and was vast but insufficiently staffed.

In 1935, the municipality of Kavala, and the then mayor Mr. Mich. Lolidis, allotted one of the most beautiful buildings in the town, the 'Faliro', for the housing of the antiquities. After the necessary preparations, therefore, the 'Faliro' became the first museum of Kavala. However, following the outbreak of the Second World War and the departure of the Greek authorities from eastern Macedonia and Thrace, the museum came into the hands of the conquerors and was completely destroyed.

In 1945, an attempt was made to reorganize

the museum, but the task was too difficult. Things changed, however, in 1952 when the museum (by then the municipal museum) was given to the state as a gift from the municipality. Repairs and enrichment of the antiquities began whilst, at the same time, excavations were undertaken in Abdera from where many important finds have come.

44

3

In the middle of 1963, construction began on the new building which since then has housed the archaeological museum of Kavala. The coastal site of the building and the atria covers 4,500 m² and was donated by the port treasury of Kavala. On the 27th of December 1964, the exhibition of antiquities in the galleries, colonnades and atria were ready and the doors of the museum were opened to visitors.

A Brief Guide to the Museum

Corridor: Here are exhibited finds from the prehistoric settlement of Dikili Tash along with ceramic potsherds from various sites in eastern Macedonia and Thrace dated to between 3000 and 2500 BC.

Atrium A: On display here are tomb stelae, inscriptions and sculptured architectural elements from various sites across Greece, which belong to the Roman Period.

Atrium B: Exhibited here are inscriptions and sculptures, mainly from Amphipolis.

Gallery of Neapolis: This room contains finds from the sanctuary of the goddess Parthenos from the area of the old town, as well as pots, figurines and small objects from the 7th century BC up to the Hellenistic Period. At the far end of the room, important architectural elements from the temple of Parthenos have been restored.

Gallery of Amphipolis: Here can be seen finds from the Classical and Hellenistic Periods of Amphipolis. Tomb stelae, gold coins, pots etc. In one corner of the room is a representation of the burial chamber of a Macedonian tomb.

Upper Floor Gallery: In here one can see objects from the colonies of Thassos, Galepsos, Oisyme and Stryme, as well as from Abdera, Mesembria and other areas of eastern Macedonia and Thrace.

4

1. Archaeological museum
2. Interior of the museum
3. Terracotta figurine of a kore, end of the 6th century BC. From the Sanctuary of Parthenos, ancient Neapolis.
4. Marble tomb stele, second half of the 4th century BC. From Amphipolis.

Folklore Museum

The fantastic neoclassical building which houses the folklore museum of Kavala is located on Philippou street.

It must have been built in the first decade of 1900 and the first owner was the tobacco trader Zachos Zachou. From 1919 until 1953 it was the site of the National Bank, while in 1986 it became the property of the municipality who used it to house the folklore museum of the town. On the ground floor of the building are the exhibition by the Thassiot sculptor Vagis Polygnotos and the hall of modern art. The upper floor of the museum contains a collection of rare birds from the area of the Nestos.

*1. The folklore museum, built along neoclassical lines.
2,3,4 and 5. Galleries within the museum.*

PHILIPPI

Ancient Theatre - Forum - Commercial forum
Baptistery & Church of Agia Lydia

Philippi is one of the most important towns of eastern Macedonia, with her acropolis set on a conical hill which separates from the mountainous mass of ancient Orbelos and descends to the rich plain which ends at the foot of the gold-bearing Pangaion mountain. Before the arrival of Greek colonists to the area of Philippi, there was a Neolithic settlement close to the spring of Dikili Tash, two kilometres east of the town. This first habitation continued after the Neolithic Age and, as finds prove, for many centuries. The prehistoric culture of Philippi had similarities to that of the Cretans, the Thessalians, the Aegean isalnders and the people of the Balkans. The fertile land and the gold mines attracted Greek colonists from Thassos who came over under the leadership of the exiled Athenian rhetorician and politician, Kallistratos, and built a small town by the name of Dato. This colony was characterized from the outset as being of special importance. During Macedonian rule, Philippi was one of the towns of the Empire which had important privileges. However, the population, and the town's importance, declined under subse-

quent Roman rule. In October 42 BC, the town gained considerable notoriety throughout the ancient world as a result of a certain historical event -the Battle of Philippi. Outside the walls of the town, to the west, two large armies (one of Republicans and the other of the Triumvirate), fought each other and the result had an historical impact: the abolition of the Republican regime in Rome, and the appointment of the first Roman emperor, Octavian. This battle was a milestone in the history of Philippi because the Roman colonists came and settled down there for two to three centuries and, thanks to their language, administration, institutions and religion, Philippi was 'transformed' into a completely Roman town.

The religious doctrines of the native Thracian population and the Greek colonists became mixed with those of the Romans and with the religion of the east. The cross, the symbol of this new religion, can be seen on the open-air sanctuaries of the rocks, and the inhabitants of Philippi were the first in Europe to preach this new religion.

The Ancient Theatre

At the foot of the acropolis, supported by the eastern wall of the town of Philippi, is the ancient theatre. This monumental structure was built around 356 BC by Philip II, king of Macedonia. The construction of the ancient theatre, whose dimensions place it among the largest of its kind, was part of the metamorphosis of Krenides (the old name of Philippi) into a large Macedonian town and, in time, the name 'Philippi' was taken up.

With the Roman colonization came the changing of the events and new architectural aesthetic demands which forced extensive alterations to the theatre. Some rows of seats were removed, the diameter of the orchestra was increased, the ground covered with large marble slabs and a marble parapet placed in order to protect the spectators from the wild beasts on display in the theatre during the Roman Period.

It is worth mentioning that within the ancient theatre of Philippi, the statue of a muse has been found which is now in the Louvre.

The last alterations to the ancient theatre were made around the 3rd century AD with the aim of changing the orchestra into a circular arena for animal fights, gladiatorial duels and chases. At this time, an underground corridor was also constructed which was used for the entry of the wild beasts from the underground arena. Also dated to this period are the three reliefs of Nemesis, Ares and Nike which are carved into the pilaster of the entry, the western parodos and the orchestra.

The ancient theatre of Philippi.

The Forum

The forum of Philippi is a rectangular square covered with marble slabs. On the four sides of the square, many buildings have been erected which appear to enlarge the dimensions of the monument. In the middle of the north side of the forum, there are the remains of a rectangular building which belong to the rostrum of the magistrates. Close to this is a carved circle with rays and partitions, which formed a type of game played by the ancients (similar games are carved in other places).

The Via Egnatia, the large road which connected Dyrrachion to Byzantium, was also connected to the forum via the two descending passages which survive at the ends of the northern side of the forum. On the northwestern side of the forum is a temple which consisted of a cella and a pronaos.

As far as the buildings of the western side of the forum are concerned, it is very possible that this was where the administrative authorities of the Roman colony settled. The most important of the rooms on that side are probably the following three: an elongated room on the northern end of the anteroom close to the Corinthian temple, the room whose western end forms an apse and was possibly the Curia (or senate building), and the room located close to the souhtwestern corner from which have survived many architectural elements. An inscription informs us that this building was burned down and rebuilt afterwards. In the northeastern corner of the forum is another Corinthian temple which is built symmetrical to the temple on the western side and has the same architectural structure. The arrangement of most of the buildings of the forum shows the existence of a unit plan, the largest of which was carried out in the second half of the 2nd century AD.

Philippi, the octagonal church.

The Commercial Agora

This large structure was built in the Roman period during the era of the Antonines. It is in the area between the eastern side and the middle of the south side of the forum, as we head southeast from the middle of the south colonnade.

The remains of this complex, along with the inscriptions which were found, have given enough evidence to allow the identification of this building as the Roman commercial agora.

The only part of the agora that has survived is the northern part which has been incorporated into the church by a Byzantine architect and forms the monumental entrance to it's northern aisle.
On the eastern side of the central entrance is a base in the shape of an altar which has an honorary inscription written in Greek.

Statues and honorary monuments which once existed, along with the games carved into the plaques for any idle individuals, show how busy the market place really was, all the town trade gathered here.

1. Honorary inscription in the shape of an altar.
2. Archaeological museum of Philippi.
3. View of the commercial agora.
4. The cell of the Apostle Paul.
5. The ancient Acropolis of Philippi.

rivers, lakes or other natural water reserves. All baptisteries had an external and internal part. The external was where the preparation for baptism were held, the covenant of Christ, the catechism and the confession of the faith. In the internal building, or fotistirio, was the font.

The baptistery of Agia Lydia is exactly as mentioned above and has an impressive entrance, changing rooms for the women, a font and, in general, is an architectural masterpiece. In the grounds of the baptistery, which nowadays cover 28,000 m², are access roads and accommodation for visitors. Since 1974, when work was completed, it has formed a major attraction for thousands of Christians from all over the world.

The Baptistery and Church of Agia Lydia

West of ancient Philippi is the Baptistery of Agia Lydia who was the first Greek female and European to be baptized by the Apostle Paul in this area. The old Christians usually baptized in the countryside, mainly where there was water;

Top: the church of Agia Lydia.
Bottom: The impressive baptistery of Agia Lydia.
Right: The Zygaktis river where Lydia was baptized.

The exquisite town of Kavala waits for the visitor to reveal her hidden treasures. It is a town where past and present are interwoven and create a fascinating atmosphere. Her charms are so numerous as to be enthralling and time seems to pass very quickly.

Dozens of alleyways and shops, both traditional and modern, maintain elements which make them special. Buildings with unique architecture which catch the eye and mind while one tries to delimit the unbelievable beauty of their construction. Parks and squares which await the weary wanderer and the town's inhabitants.

THE TOWN

The marvellous port which, one would think, has been there since the beginning; an integral part of the surrounding beauty -but what to see, and what to admire first?!

Words may not be enough to describe the feelings, but it is certain that the visitor to Kavala will fall in love with the town at first glance.

The tour of the town is a fascinating walk; a route through her history. Imposing monuments and ancient ruins revive pictures of the past, whilst modern, renovated buildings present a view of the modern life of the town.

Panoramic view of Kavala.

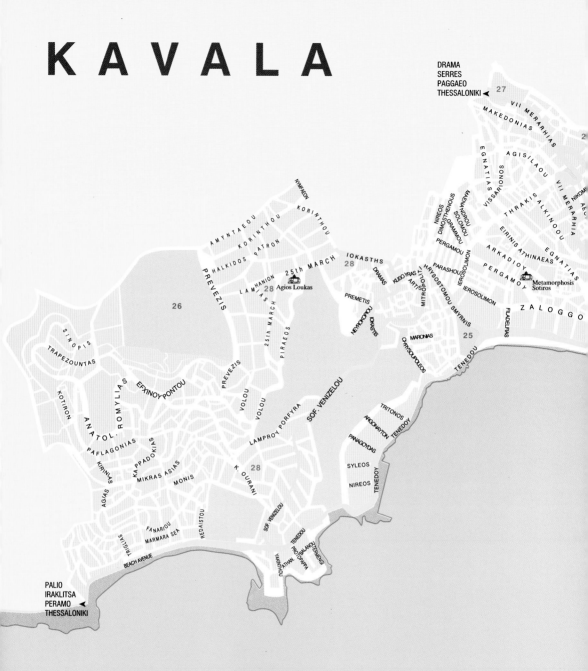

K A V A L A

DRAMA
SERRES
PAGGAEO
THESSALONIKI ◄ 27

VII MERARHIAS

2

MAKEDONIAS

AGIS/LAOU VII MERARHIA

SONORIOU

VISSARIOU

THRAKIS

NIKOMI

AEG

EGNATIAS

MYKENANDROU

NIREOS

DIMOSTHENOUS

SOLOMOU

GRAMMOU

PERGAMOU

SALKINOOU

EIRINIS

ATHINAEAS

EGNATIAS

ARKADIOY

PERGAMO

NYMFAEON

KORINTHOU

AMYNTAEOU

KORINTHOU

KORINTHOU

HALKIDOS

PATRON

PREVEZIS

LAMHANION

25th MARCH

IOKASTHS

28

DRAMAS

PARASHOU

IEROSOLIMON

IEROSOLIMON

FILADELFIAS

Metamorphosis
Sotiros

ZALOGGO

28 Agios Loukas

25th MARCH

PREMETIS

KUSOYRAS

ARTPOLI

MITROPOLI

HRYSOSTOMOU

SMYRNIS

26

NEFROKOPOU

IONISTIS

MARONIAS

25

PIRAEOS

CHRYSOUPOLEOS

TENEDOU

SINOPIS

TRAPEZOUNTAS

PREVEZIS

TENEDOY

KOTIRON

EFXINOY PONTOU

ROMYLIAS

VOLOU

VOLOU

LAMPROY PORFYRA

SOF. VENIZELOU

TRITONOS

ARGONAYTON

TENEDOY

ANATOL.

PAFLAGONIAS

KAPPADOKIAS

K. OURANI

PANAGOYDAS

TENEDOY

KIRINIAS

MIKRAS ASIAS

28

SYLEOS

AGIAS

MONIS

SOF. VENIZELOU

NIREOS

TENEDOY

TRIGLIAS

FANARIOU

REDAISTOU

TENEDOU

PROIGOBAPA

YAKINTHOU

PROIGOBALANOY

STENIMEGI

KAVARA

MARMARA SEA

BEACH AVENUE

PALIO
IRAKLITSA
PERAMO ◄
THESSALONIKI

LEGEND

1. Museum
2. Government House
3. Swimming Pool
4. Park
5. Municipal Theatre
6. National Insurance Foundation (I.K.A.)
7. Olympic Airways

8. Bus Interchange (K.T.E.L.)
9. Telecommunications Company (O.T.E.)
10. Ferries
11. War Memorial
12. Municipal Library
13. Town Hall
14. Cultural Centre

15. Post Office

16. Municipal Market

17. Foreign Press Agency

18. Lawcourts

19. 'Kamares' Aqueduct

20. Castle

21. Imaret

22. House and Statue of Mehmet Ali

23. Customs House

24. Hospital

25. Fire Station

26. Technical College (T.E.I.)

27. Retirement Home

28. School

The Kamares

We will begin our tour from the centre of Kavala, from the Kamares aqueduct. It is a colossal construction, one of the many works of Suleiman the Magnificent, and was built around AD 1550 on the 'tracks' of the 'long wall' which had been built by the emperor Andronicus II Palailogus to halt the return of the Catalans to Thrace.

In addition to its defensive role, this wall was used as an aqueduct. A walkway existed on top of the wall along which the guards made their patrol and underneath this, inside the same wall on the side closest to the town, was arranged the aqueduct which brought water from the spring which is along the path on the way to old Kavala.

After the catastrophe suffered by the town in the 15th century, the old aqueduct was demolished. The Sultan himself, then raised, on the site of the old 'wall', the new aqueduct, which was known as the 'Kamares' or 'Arches' so that the town could be supplied with water from a spring on the opposite summit, in the modern quarter of Timios Stavros (Sougiolou). The aqueduct descended from the spring and, passing along the top of the Kamares, reached the old town. The construction incorporated sixty arches of four different sizes, the largest of which was 52 metres tall.

1. *The statue of the lion which stands imperiously in front of the Kamares is a representation of the one in Amphipolis.*
2. *The shipyard of the town.*
3. *The Kamares, the distinctive monument and symbol of Kavala, founded in 1530*

Town Hall

The town hall of Kavala, on Kyprou street, is possibly one of the most impressive buildings of the town. Its architectural style is unique and completely 'foreign' to the area of Kavala. It is often said to be a miniature of the tower of Hungary and must have been built at the end of the 1890s.

It belonged to the Hungarian tobacco trader Baron Pierre Erzoch. In 1921, it was sold by his son, Maurice Erzoch, to the 'Tobacco Company of the Eastern Sea and Beyond Ltd.'. In 1937, the building was put up for compulsory auction on account of the debts of the Eastern Tobacco Company Ltd., and was bought by the municipality of Kavala in order to house the Town Hall, where it still stands.

The internal organization of the rooms of the building makes a lasting impression on the visitor where, in the past, brilliant society events were held.

The Small Town Hall

In the same street as the town hall, next to the monastery of the Lazarists, stands the small town hall of Kavala.

Within the building is a Turkish property deed from 1906 which may be identical to the year of construction. It belonged to the German, Baron Adolfo de Szolnay Wiz, from whom it was bought, in 1925, by an American tobacco company, and later became the property of the Glen Tobacco Company and, immediately after, ownership fell to the tobacco trader, Nikos Petridis.

Today, the building is the property of the municipality of Kavala and a number of public services are housed within it.

1. The impressive building
of the main town hall of Kavala.
2. The imposing church of Agios Pavlos.
3. The Byzantine Antiquities Unit.

² The Holy Church of Agios Pavlos

The Holy Church of Agios Pavlos (Saint Paul), the patron saint of the town, is one of the most imposing and magnificent churches in the area. Built in the centre of Kavala, it honours the founder of the church of Philippi who made this town his first port of call in the whole of Europe. The plans for the church were begun in 1900 by a team of devout Christians. In 1905, the then Metropolitan of Xanthi, Joachim Sgouros laid the foundation stone. The Greek community had previously asked for the consent of the Turkish administration under whose rule the town was then subject. It should be noted here that this building is a three-aisled, domed basilica and was used as the first church of the Apostle Paul. There are hagiographs of Renaissance technique made by monks from Mount Athos, as well as a number of Byzantine ones.

In a room next to the church, the Eucharist is held which marks the continuation of the real love of the apostle of the Nations towards the Christians. On the day of the feast, which overlaps with the liberation of Kavala, a festive, holy service is held and the procession of the icon through the streets of the town is made.

The Byzantine Antiquities Unit

On Kyprou street, one finds the present-day Byzantine Antiquities Unit, in the building formerly known as the Megaro Tokkos which was built in 1879 by the tobacco trader D. Tokkos, whose name can be seen on a relief inscription above the lintel. In 1911, Nikolaos Tokkos sold this house to Theodoros Rakintzis on behalf of the Charitable Brotherhood of Gentlemen of Kavala.

In the past, the building was used as a consulate whilst, after the liberation of Kavala from the Turks, it hosted the Town Hall until 1937 when it became the privately-owned building it is today.

Agios Silas

The Agios Silas monastery stands on the saddle of the hill, at the foot of which lies the charming town of Kavala. On the main gate is the Byzantine inscription HOLY MONASTERY OF THE APOSTLE SILAS'.

The monastery was founded by the Metropolitan Chrysostomos Chatzistavrou, who later became archbishop of Athens, and who was uprooted from Ephesus in Ionia along with the refugees from Pontus, eastern Thrace and Asia Minor.

The foundation of the Agios Silas monastery was a result of the desire to have it' s spiritual light create leaps and deep emotion in the hearts of all people who know how to inspire themselves with the ideals of Orthodoxy. However, before the foundation of the monastery by Chrysostomos, the hill of Agios Silas was passed by the Apostle Paul and his companions who stopped there to rest. This is how the legend is told and how it is represented on a marble stele in front of the katholikon.

In 1937, after considerable donations from the Christians of Kavala, the first small church rose. Later in 1956, the majestic stone-built katholikon was consecrated along with the rest of the buildings of the complex. As far as the yard of the monastery is concerned, immediately after the entry, to the right on the raised area, stands the chapel of Agios Anthimos. Further on, one sees the old marble architectural elements of holy churches and an area with birds and animals of the wood. Directly after this is a stone fountain, opposite which can be seen the small bell-tower with its magnificent bells. Next to it, and in front of the guest quarters, is the large reception hall with the vivid icons of the Second Coming and a small display of relics and important books.

On the same side are the abbot's quarters and the cells of the fathers. Below the guest quarters stands a fountain and the icon-stand of Golgotha, whilst the whole place is covered in elaborately worked schist.

The Holy monastery of Agios Silas.

The centre of the complex is dominated by the grand katholikon of the monastery with its majestic dome and, high up, the dazzlingly white cross which captures the eye standing out, as it does, from the lofty pine trees. The interior of the church is magnificent, the decoration simple and unaffected. The bodies of the saints are kept here. Finally, in the yard of the monastery is a monument in honour of the heroes who fell during the liberation of the nation. At one time, all visitors who wished to see the Agios Silas monastery had to ascend on foot from Kavala, but today it is possible to travel as far as the yard of the monastery by car.

The Monastery of the Lazarists

This monastery, also lying along Kyprou street, must have been built between 1880 and 1892. The ground was sold or given as a gift by Baron Wiz thanks to the presence of the Catholic priest Etienne Zougla in Kavala. It was used as a monastery for the Lazarists and later for the French consulate. The whole building has architectural elements of various styles including neoclassical influence in the spirit of the times. As far as the pylon is concerned, it ends in a niche where the little statuette of Agios Vikentios, the founder of the orders of the Lazarists, is housed, and it must have been built by the same craftsman who built the municipal tobacco warehouse.

The Municipal Library

The Megali Leschi, or Large Club, today's municipal library, is at 12 Kyprou street. In 1909, the estate changed hands from the girl's school of Kavala (which was on its northern side) to the committee of the Charitable Brotherhood of Gentlemen, for the purpose of building the Club for the Greek Community of Kavala, with the condition that the height of the new building not obstruct the view to the girls' school from the south. The building has been restored recently under the supervision of the Byzantine Antiquities Unit and, as mentioned above, now houses the municipal library. There are often lectures, art exhibitions, musical events and congresses held here.

The Tobacco Warehouse

This building was built at the end of the first decade of the 1900s as a tobacco warehouse for the Turkish tobacco trader, Kizi Mimin. The building now belongs to the municipality of Kavala and hosts cultural events of the town, such as theatre, cultural society clubs and museums with exhibitions on the history of the town. The folklore museum of Kavala and the museum of Polygnotos Vagis will also be transferred here. The building has been restored externally and its architectural and decorative beauties have been stressed thanks to the work of the Byzantine Antiquities Unit.

1. The building of the municipal library.
2. The tobacco warehouse on Kapnergati square.
3. The monastery of the Lazarists.

The Port

Kavala has the most charming and delightful port in the northern Aegean. A large port which extends its embrace to all ships, - commercial and passenger. Since antiquity it has been a pole of attraction for colonists, conquerors and tradesmen, and was the first port in Europe where the Apostle Paul landed. In the middle of the 19th century, foreign companies acknowledged that it was a real 'jewel' with regards to business

Today the arrangement of the port allows for the docking of large commercial ships as well as any passing cruise liners. It is the port from which the ships set out for Thassos, Limnos, Lesbos and Samothrace, and a stopping off point for those liners making longer hauls.

Pictures of the port of Kavala.

Another important fact to mention is the existence of the nautical societies, ΟΘΑΚ and NOK, which teach sailing and take part in competitions in Greece and abroad. Above all, however, the port of Kavala is a landing place for trawlers and, in general, all manner of fishing vessels. Until a few years ago, across from the port, in the place where the fishing boats dock, was the fish market of Kavala where one could find fresh fish all day.

The area has also been used for various events.

In the afternoons, but mostly on Sundays, aspiring fishermen gather on the little pier of NOK, and make an unbelievably charming scene.

A walk around the port is considered one of the most attractive in Kavala. Delightful street sellers, the theme park and the palm trees combine in this exquisite area of the town.

6 THE OLD

The area of Panagia is an attractive, traditional and well-maintained area of town which draws the eye of the visitor from the very first moment. It emits a magnetism that originates from the blending of past and present, a fact which influences and touches the majority of the inhabitants even today. The many monuments are silent witnesses to the creation, flourishing and revival of the town from antiquity up to 1864.

All the history of Kavala happened here in the area of Panagia. Witnesses of all those events that marked the times for the inhabitants of Neapolis, Christoupolis and Kavala.

TOWN

The fortress - The Church of Panajia- The Lighthouse

It is the first bit of land one sees from the sea on approaching the town. At one time there were walls around this old town, lain for the first time in the 5th century BC, which were built on top of by the Byzantines, the Venetians and finally the Turkish. In the centre was a castle that we can still admire today and there were at least two entrances to the town, one of which has survived intact.

Today the old town with the paved alleyways, the Imaret, the Panagia and the lighthouse, creates a wonderful scene, which you would think was straight out of a fairy tale.

The Fortress

Imperious and awesome, the fortress together with the Kamares, are the symbols of Kavala. It dominates the town and is the first thing that catches the visitor's eye whilst, at the same time, giving one an idea of what the town will be like.

The fortress known locally as Frourio is just one part of the walls of the old town.

There is no doubt that it is the most intriguing element of the upper part of the town and has, naturally, survived up to today.

The fortress was built by the Turks and Venetians in AD 1425. The walls of the town, up to 180 metres long, have an extensive history and were built in the 5th century BC with boulders of a local granite. Parts of the walls still survive in many places -mainly in the west- of this quarter.

These walls were expanded and repaired by the Byzantines, and in AD 1306, the emperor of Byzantium, Andronicus II Paliologus, built the 'Long Wall'.

The acropolis of Kavala was the last shelter and the final hope for the inhabitants of the old town from the sieges and attacks of the pirates and other enemies.

The construction follows the line of the land and consists of an external yard with three towers and two entrances. It is the place where today one finds the small open-air theatre of Frourio.

The interior, the safer part, consists of a large water tank, an arsenal -which was later used as a prison- and the central tower for the last line of defence.

The battlements were reached by small, periodic stairways which can still be seen. This interior part had a length of 90 metres, a width of 3.6 metres and circumference of about 200 metres, whilst the central tower was eighteen metres tall.

Today it is one of the first spots that 'should' be visited because from here one can take the most wonderful pictures.

The ascent to the fortress may be a bit tiring but the route and the sites one will see on the way up are the greatest reward. During the summer, in the small open-air theatre mentioned above, many concerts are held and plays performed.

The area is one which especially inspires artists and, when the air is clean, one can clearly see Thassos, the peninsulas of Peramos and Mount Athos, and even Samothrace.

The castle of the town stands imposing and imperious.

The Imaret

On the Theodorou Pavlidou road, in the western sector of the old town is the 'Imaret'; the amazing jewel of Islamic architecture. Built in 1817 by Mehmet Ali, very close to the location of the ancient sanctuary of Parthenos, it initially functioned as a seminary and poorhouse as well as a boarding school with eight teachers.

At the same time, every noon in the large mess-hall, the poor inhabitants of Kavala could find soup, pilau bread and, twice a week, a piece of meat in addition. 'The Imaret' housed about 600 boarders in the summer and 300 in winter and its maintenance costs amounted to 8,000 gold sovereigns a year.

The money for these costs came from the income of the Pasha through his exploitation of Thassos, about 400,000 piastres a year, together with a personal donation.

The building stretches over a large area of the peninsula and the inscription of ownership is on a built-in lintel of one of the entrances.

There are three atria, surrounded by many smaller and larger areas. The school stopped functioning in 1912, while the poorhouse continued until 1923 when the 'Imaret' closed for ever. As a result the building was abandoned and some of it began to collapse. Today, despite the fact that it is still the property of Egypt, you can visit it and see some of its rooms.

There is a refreshment bar operating throughout the year where you can listen to authentic Egyptian music.

The House of Mehmet Ali

In 1769, the founder of the last Egyptian dynasty, Mehmet Ali, was born in Kavala. He lived here for many years, in the town he loved and to which he gave many benefits. He was the father of the notorious Ibrahim of the Greek revolution and his rise from the moment he joined the army and his remarkable carrier are well known.

The port recognized him as Pasha of Egypt in 1807 and to thank him, Egypt offered him the island of Thassos as a hereditary gift. To honour him, in 1934, the Greeks of Egypt erected a wonderful bronze equestrian statue, the work of the sculptor Dimitriadis, in front of his paternal home at the southeastern edge of the old town, the unveiling of which was performed on the 6th of December 1940.

The family house of Mehmet Ali, in which he was born and grew up, was built in 1720 and still survives in remarkable condition.

It was restored before the Second World War and is today a museum. It has two floors, a stable and a kitchen and the upper floor holds the harem, the personal rooms of the Pasha and the room of his favoured one. Finally, there is a guard who guides visitors around the house and expects a small tip.

The Church of Panajia

The Panajia is one of the most charming in Kavala and has a delightful view of the sea. It is in the southeastern part of the town between the square of Mehmet Ali and the lighthouse on the edge of the small peninsula. In the past there was a nunnery here of which the bell-tower and some icons from the iconostasis have survived. Agios Philotheos of Kavala set out from here and lived for many years. The church which stands here today was begun around 1965 on the site of the nunnery. A remarkable point, worthy of note, is the fact that a consecration was never performed on account of the altar changing positions. The only service performed was a small one by the then metropolitan, Chrysostomos. The old church was a basilica, whilst the present one is a Byzantine cruciform with a dome. In the interior of the church are two chapels dedicated to Agios Fanourios and Agios Philotheos, as well as a reception hall.

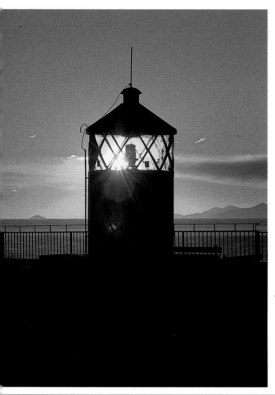

The Lighthouse

One of the most famous and wonderful areas of Panagia is that where the lighthouse stands. A bright beacon to the ships and a pole of attraction for inhabitants of Kavala as well as for the visitors, it has a fascinating view with the whole town stretched out before us with a beauty that is difficult to put into words. A few metres further on from the lighthouse is the old primary school which still functions whilst, directly beneath the lighthouse, rise the famous rocks of Panagia. The massive, sheer cliffs are ideal for those who want to sit and get lost in the azure of the sea and the uniqueness of the landscape. In summer, many are those who prefer this spot for swimming and fishing, and some of the more daring ones extract mussels. The area of the lighthouse is one of the most interesting in Panagia and one can imagine it as a place where all the secrets of the past are hidden. It also happens to be an ideal spot for taking pictures of the whole town.

FISHING VILLAGES & BEACHES

Palio - Nea Iraklitsa - Nea Peramos

Kavala has the most beautiful beaches which are one of the main things that capture the heart of her visitors. Velvety with crystal-clear water, they attract many people from the neighbouring prefectures and, naturally, tourists from all over the world. Small cliffs, rocks and crystal-clear waters are the things one will find on the tour to the nearby coastal resorts and villages located to the west outside town. For those who like their journey to be easy, we mention here the more organized and busier beaches, but for those who prefer more isolated and empty beaches, these are not difficult to find. A little exploration of the cliffs to the left of the road which leads to the coastal resorts will help in the discovery of ideal places for swimming.

Two kilometres from the centre of Kavala is

The golden beach of Tosca.

the organized, sandy beach of Kalamitsa. It is about 500 metres from the 'Lousi' hotel and has many changing rooms, showers and playgrounds. One kilometre further on is the beach of Batis. This is also an organized beach, belonging to the Greek Tourist Board (EOT), and has changing rooms, showers, a bar, a restaurant and playgrounds, and is ideal for water sports and 'beach tennis'. The sea here is of the cleanest and deepest in the surrounding area. Another three kilometres along, as we approach Palio, another wonderful beach, Tosca, stretches out before us. Here we find the hotel of the same name and a small and relatively quiet beach with a good restaurant. The sea is clean and the beach is covered with pebbles, Whilst on the left and right are cliffs for diving.

The beautiful beach of Kalamitsa

Palio

The idyllic and very attractive resort of Palio is the traditional haunt of the few wealthy people of Kavala and has become a cosmopolitan centre of summer tourism. There are rooms for rent here as well as wonderful tavernas, cafés, bars and clubs, but mainly it is the good sandy beaches and clean water that attracts the countless visitors.

The combination of the mountains and the sea make Palio one of the most fascinating spots of Kavala.

Palio, one of the traditional resorts of Kavala.

Nea Iraklitsa

The coastal resort of Nea Iraklitsa is one of the most charming villages of the area. Twelve kilometres from Kavala, it gazes eastwards out to sea and is surrounded by bushy hills which become completely green in spring. It also has one of the largest and cleanest sandy beaches.

Nearby, on the small scenic cape completely covered in pine trees, is a small pier which was in use before the road was completed, traffic being then via the sea, and an exquisite little port which primarily serves the fishermen.

The development and works carried out in recent years have made this area the preferred choice of the people of Kavala, as well as those from neighbouring prefectures, for careless Sunday outings. There are fish tavernas, restaurants, cafés, bars and sweet shops with amazing doughnuts all along the coast as well as many hotels and a large number of rooms for rent which, during the summer season, are crammed with people. Just before we enter Nea Iraklitsa, there is an organized camping ground, the 'ESTELLA'.

It's beach is delightful, very well equipped, and it has a bar and one of the finest restaurants

On the 23rd of August, Nea Iraklitsa celebrates the nine days of Panagia and for one week the atmosphere becomes festive.

The fishing village of Nea Iraklitsa with its impressive beach.

Nea Peramos

Immediately after Nea Iraklitsa, and sixteen kilometres from Kavala, is Nea Peramos; a beautiful coastal village with marvellous beaches and picturesque fish tavernas.
A short distance before Nea Peramos is the little port of Eleftheres from where the amateur and professional fishermen set out in boats, caïques and trawlers.

In the village, as well as in the idyllic surrounding landscape, one can find hotels, rooms for rent and camping grounds which serve a large number of tourists, especially during the summer season.

In Nea Peramos and the quaint little village of Eleftheres, located in the mountainous part of Peramos, are vine yards which yield the famous grapes used for the production of wine. Along the main road of Nea Peramos stretches the velvet sandy beach with its completely clean waters. To the west of the village, on a tree-lined hill, is the old castle -a silent witness to another time. The view from here is astounding, with the whole gulf of Nea Peramos and the peninsula of Vrassida (which has fantastic beaches and unlimited fishing), stretching out before us.
A short distance from the castle are the well known beaches of Ammolofi, a fascinating place with the cleanest sea in the area.
It is a spot which draws for the people from the neighbouring prefectures of Drama and Serres.

The vast beach of Nea Peramos is not only ideal for swimming but also for sea sports.

CHRYSSOUPOLIS

Keramoti - The Delta and Narrows of the Nestos River

East of Kavala, roughly twenty eight kilometres away, is Chryssoupolis, a large market town surrounded by a fertile plain crossed by the Nestos river. The old name for Chryssoupolis was Sari (Gold) Samban because it must once have belonged to an important landowner called Samban. However, because it was surrounded by marshes, the owner of the chiftlik (a large estate) contracted a local form of malaria and his face turned yellow. As far as antiquity records, the Via Egnatia crossed the Nestos river to the northeast of Chryssoupolis via the Roman stone bridge which was in roughly the same position as today's bridge close to the village of Toxotes. Chryssoupolis, however, was once an important crossroads, and this is apparent from the large number of inns which make up today's historical centre of the town, and also from the fact that many people have businesses such as bakeries, grocery stores, carriage services; in short, everything that a traveller could need. With the arrival of the refugees, Chryssoupolis expanded, with her inhabitants coming primarily from Asia Minor and Pontos, but a large number also from the Thracians and Sarakatsani, though these were restricted to the villages of the plain. The newly-established market town grew and

The narrows of the Nestos river.

became a strong, important, economical power by virtue of it's agriculture. It is one of the areas which give support to the markets of Kavala and Xanthi. Chryssoupolis may not be picturesque, but she is surrounded by engaging natural beauty. Beside her, the Nestos river flows with its verdant banks; ideal areas for picnics and walks. The wood which once surrounded the river was one of the densest and richest in Europe, in terms of flora and fauna. Today, only a small part survives which is enclosed by the forestry commision who protect it as 'the apple of the state's eye'. The large lake of Alaca Göl is also exquisite. The name is Turkish and means 'Multicoloured Lake', though the locals call it 'Fake Lake' as it is basically a swamp. Myths and legends relate how it's depths hide a small settlement which sank because of the earthquakes. In the plain of Chryssoupolis, among the small and large villages, the coastal village of Keramoti stands out. Besides the villages of the plain, those up in the mountains are also wonderful and it is from here that many inhabitants have been moved to Chryssoupolis. Finally, to the west of Chryss-oupolis lies the 'Alexander the Great' airport which even serves flights from abroad.

LEGEND
Town Hall
Bus Interchaange
National Bank
National Health Unit
Inland Revenue
General Bank
Rural Police
Commercial Bank

⑨ Police
⑩ Post Office
⑪ Cultural Society
⑫ Macedonia Thrace Bank
⑬ Electricity Company
⑭ Ionian Bank
⑮ Telecommunications Company
⑯ Agricultural Bank
⑰ Fire Station

ΚΛΙΜΑΚΑ: 1 : 5,700

Keramoti

About ten kilometres southwest of Chryssoupolis is the picturesque coastal village of Keramoti. It is the second port after Kavala which connects with Thassos. Despite the fact that it could be characterized as a fishing village, as the majority if it's inhabitants are involved in fishing, it attracts a large number of tourists every year, especially during the summer. Keramoti has one of the largest beaches with fine sand and crystal clear waters. From high up it looks like an island because the only part that is connected with the rest of the mainland is a bridge at the entrance to the village. One of the most idyllic landscapes is Faros, a verdant area, covered in pine trees, on the edge of the peninsula. Many choose this particular spot to spend their Sunday having picnics, fishing and swimming. The port of Keramoti is charming and ideal for walks, and every year, on the 6th of August when the village celebrates the Grace of the Saviour, it becomes very crowded. Alongside the main road, but still close to the port, there are fish tavernas and watering-holes where one can eat the freshest fish. The sea in the area is one of the richest in terms of fish and other sea creatures. In Keramoti, the cultivation of mussels is also organized and these mussels are considered the most delicious in the whole prefecture.

The picturesque village of Keramoti is ideal, especially during the summer months, for those who love fishing.

South of Keramoti is the island of **Thassopoula**. It is barren, rocky and difficult to approach because of the strong current, but despite this, many times it provides 'shelter' for the fishermen when bad weather catches them out on the sea. Keramoti is an ideal pace for holidays and can cater for a large number of visitors because it has hotels, apartments and rooms for rent. It is also the only place where one can spend quiet holidays without a lack of entertainment opportunities.

The pier of the port of Keramoti.

The Delta of the Nestos River

One of the most fascinating areas of Chryssoupolis, and of the whole prefecture, is the delta of the Nestos river. An area not only idyllic with vibrant colours throughout the year, but also of great ecological importance. It is a Utopian wilderness where one can admire the magnificence of nature.

The delta of the Nestos river is southeast of Chryssoupolis, outside the village of Nea Karya, but in order to reach it one has first to go to the forestry commission, close to the Nestos river, and then one can proceed after having been informed by the chief forester which road to follow.

The route may be a little difficult but it is, at the same time, unbelievably captivating, winding among trees of various kinds, flowers, bushes and many other kind of greenery grows. As far as the point where the river meets the sea, the scene is unique. The banks are completely green and the pattern of the streams is amazing.

The islet formed from the sand brought down by the river, is of a strange beauty and a place where seagulls find shelter. As far as the banks are concerned, they are a place where the wild animals of the area go to quench their thirst. Early in the morning one can find their tracks close to the water. The delta of the Nestos river is a beloved place of the fishermen of the area and some of them keep their boats there.

The delta is also of great importance from an ecological aspect, because it is a place where many rare migratory birds rest and where one can find some of the rarest plants in the world. Together with the narrows of the river, the delta makes a heaven on earth of the area.

The delta of the Nestos river is one of the few natural paradises in Greece.

The Narrows of the Nestos River

At the border between the prefectures of Kavala and Xanthi, outside the village of Toxotes, are the narrows of the Nestos river. A paradise hidden in the mountains. Another world which, once you get to know it, remains for always in your mind.

At the beginning of the climb is a huge plane tree and cool water runs out of the heart of the mountain. Immediately after this is a narrow stone pathway carved along the giant rock which hangs massively over the river. The view offered by the river as it runs along is truly amazing.

The alternately visible sand in the shallows and those hidden in the depths of the river, look like rare formations that can only have been created by some mysterious being.

Shoals of trout swim stubbornly against the stream and the wanderer feels that there is no more absolute union between man and nature at this particular moment that he experiences.

The ascent becomes increasingly beautiful, whilst the train tracks stretch like a snake and the tunnels carved into the mountain appear to almost furtively conceal it. On the opposite side of the river, small sandy beaches can be seen as well as ideal areas for walking and resting. During the route, small descending pathways lead to the river. The trees here are now so dense that it is almost impossible to see the blue of the sky. The journey up can last a whole day but for those who would like to get another view of the route, there are organized walks and excursions by train which start from the town of Drama.

This dreamy place, only about fifty kilometres from Kavala, is one of the areas that the visitor should not miss.

The narrows of the Nestos river take their turn in composing the earthly paradise of Kavala.

9

ELEFTHEROUPOLIS

Pangaion - Agios Dimitrios Monastery
Ikosifinissa Pangaion Monastery - Panagia Pangaiotissa
Nunnery - Ypapantis tou Christou Nunnery

Between the Symbolon and Pangaion mountains, lies Eleftheroupolis, about twenty kilometres from Kavala. It is a market town in which the old and new bind harmoniously together and one would think that time runs backwards. The first time this town is mentioned, is when she was still called Pravi -in 1212. Since then, she has lived through many periods and her history is more or less the same as that for the rest of the region. During the years of Turkish occupation Eleftheroupolis was the place where the cannon balls of the Turks were made as well as other armaments. Also from this town came the famous warrior of 1821, Nikotsaros, who battled against the Turks. The town is also known from the battle which took place here between the Greeks and Bulgarians in 1913. Extremely picturesque are the old houses with the strange tiled roofs and the narrow alleyways with the beautiful cafés.

The large tobacco warehouses are imposing and, though they remain closed today, are a reminder of a time when Eleftheroupolis was a large tobacco processing centre. Equally impressive are the huge building of the secondary school, the stadium, the town hall and the government house. The church which stands out in Eleftheroupolis is that of Agios Nikolaos, built in the 17th century, which is half below ground because, during the years of the Turkish occupation, it was not permitted to build churches in visible places. A little further north of Eleftheroupolis is the community of Eleftheres, built on the site of ancient Eion and the later Byzantine Eleftheroupolis of which ruins survive.

The baths of Eleftheres are also famous with their curative waters which heal many illnesses, even chronic ones. It should not be forgotten that Eleftheroupolis is the starting point for unforgettable excursions to the verdant slopes of Mt. Pangaion.

Panoramic view of Eleftheroupolis.

Pangaion

The Pangaion mountain, the legendary and gold-bearing mountain, stands imposingly among the mountains of Lekani, Falakron, Menikion, Kerdylion and Symbolon. Vast, completely green with sharp rocky summits of which the highest reaches some 1,956 metres, it has an unbelievable charm. It has been wooded since antiquity with beech trees, oaks, firs, huge plane trees and chestnuts and has gorges and slopes full of gold and silver. According to legend, the summits of Mount Pangaion are where Dionysus, god of Thrace and Phrygia, established his oracle and sanctuary, together with the Maenads and the Sileni, to enrich the nature there. The mountain priests of the Satyrs, the Vissoi, were in charge of looking after the sanctuary and the oracle and they made sacrifices of white horses. There was also a priestess of the temple who gave ambiguous oracles, like Pythia. Remains of the Dionysiac-Orphic dances of the Maenads and the Sileni can be seen in the custom of the Arapedes which is revived in Nikisiani on Mt. Pangaion and attracts many visitors. The Arapedes are people dressed in the skins of animals or long cloaks which cover their bodies down to their calves. This custom was first started by the people in memory of the victory of Alexander the Great in Asia. Later, Orpheus, son of King Oeagrus of Thrace and of Calliope (one of the seven muses) came to the Pangaion mountain. He was the first poet, the first bard inspired by the gods who, with the lyrical strength of the lyre, used to tame both men and animals. Today Mount Pangaion continues to be a dense green paradise which attracts climbers, nature lovers, hunters and simple visitors. As far as the high slopes among the summits are concerned, it is here that the wonderful monasteries are built which are an integral part of the grand design.

The charming beauty of the landscape around Kavala is indisputably taken up by the verdant Mount Pangaion.

The Ikosifinissa Pangaion Monastery

Climbing the steepest slopes of the Pangaion mountain and following a twisting road which winds up like a snake built among the lush green summits, brings us to the holy monastery of Ikosifinissa Pangaion. The wonderful scene is completed by the huge beech trees and chestnuts which seem to hide the monastery away for protection as they did during the difficult years of mass destruction. The founder of the monastery was the Blessed Germanos who, around 1,500 years ago, was a monk at the Prodromos monastery in the Holy Land. During a period of concentration and prayers, the Virgin appeared to him and asked him to build a monastery on the Pangaion mountain in Macedonia in her honour.

With the help of an angel who appeared before him, he was led to the place where Panagia wanted him to build the monastery. There he found, while he was digging the foundations of the monastery, two crosses with which he worked wonders. The fame of the monastery was the reason that almost all the invaders wanted to destroy it. The first time it was destroyed was in 1507 by the wild Turk toparch, who was exasperated by the monks of the monastery because they presented problems, through their teachings and catechisms, to the Turks' attempts to Islamize the natives.

However, the rage of the Bulgarians against the monastery during the Macedonian war is also astonishing. This first happened in 1917, when a large number of Bulgarian troops arrived at the monastery led by four officers who had made plans to pillage the handmade icon of the Virgin and to destroy the monastery. One of the officers who entered the church and touched the wonder-working icon of Panagia, was thrown by an invisible force on to the marble column to the left. As a result of this blow, he broke his head and died instantly. His blood, boot and pistol remain imprinted on the marble of the floor of the church to this day.

The Bulgarians attacked the monastery for the second time in 1943, and after having killed many monks, they set fire to the monastery. The only part of the monastery that survived was the katholikon and that was a miracle. As far as the icon of Panagia is concerned, it was taken by inhabitants of Nikisiani who kept it hidden until it was restored to the monastery in 1946 after the liberation. Today the beauty and charm of the monastery attract thousands of pilgrims from all over Greece. The divine service that is held, together with the sweet psalmody of the double choir, has the mood and style of that from Byzantium and Mount Athos. Besides the wonderful cruciform shape, the church has a dome which is similar to those on Mount Athos and is also surrounded by a large number of cells, chapels and other buildings. The monastery of Ikosifinissa Pangaion is one of the most important 'treasures' of the area that a visitor should see.

The monastery of Ikosifinissa.

The Agios Dimitrios Monastery

Apparently trapped within an idyllic ravine, in Nikisiani Pangaion, is the Agios Dimitrios monastery. Within this monastery is the holy water of Agia Varvara, a spring from which cool water spouts forth from the depths of the Pangaion mountain. The chapel of Agios Dimitrios was once here which was maintained very devoutly, by a family of shepherds who watered their flocks at the location of the 'spouting water'. The building works of the monastery began in 1974 and included a structure with cells for the monks, a guest house, a refectory and a reception hall. Today, expansion works are being carried out but this does not preclude the hosting of magnificent ceremonies. A special moment for the monastery of Agios Dimitrios is the enactment of the route to Golgotha on Good Friday when the deposition of the cross is held on the hill opposite the monastery where there is a majestic cross. The monastery is a brilliant shrine and is one of the most beautiful on the mountain.

The Ypapantis tou Christou Nunnery

The Ypapantis tou Christou (Candlemas of Christ) nunnery is one of the largest. It follows the old calendar and was built in 1955 on ruins of the village of Dranova, (formerly Chortokopi), whose inhabitants are now all settled close to the plain. The landscape is one of the most beautiful on Pangaion and the view of the nunnery is exquisite. The location of the buildings of the nunnery was chosen by the mother superior, Fevrouia, after a previous vision. With the assistance of the believers the nunnery was completed and it is now surrounded by a tall wall. In the area of the nunnery is the impressive church of Ypapantis, a three-aisled basilica which celebrates on the 2nd of February. On the day before, but also on the day of the celebration, a religious festival is held. The Ypapantis tou Christou nunnery is one of the most magnificent in mass and one of the most famous in the area.

The Panagia Pangaiotissa Nunnery

Above Chortokopi, a picturesque village of Pangaion on the top of a hill, is the wonderfully sited Panagia Pangaiotissa nunnery. The area was chosen by a Pontian family after a holy vision which revealed to them the location of the holy icon, which they brought with them from their homeland and which is still on the hill where the nunnery is situated. Construction began in 1979 and new guest rooms are continually added to its complex. Despite the fact that it is for nuns, it functions with the religious observances of the monasteries of Mount Athos. The church in which the service is held is dedicated to Kimissis tis Theotkou (the Assumption of the Virgin) and celebrates on the 15th of August. The complex of the nunnery includes guest rooms, a kitchen and workshops for the nuns.

1. The Panagia Pangaiotissa nunnery.
2. The Ypapantis tou Christou nunnery.

10 THASSOS

THASSOS
(Limenas)
Skala Rachoniou
Glyfada
Makryammos
Chryssi
Ammoudia
Skala
Sotiras
+
1127
Panagia
Prinos
Potamia
Maries
Kalirachi
Skala
Marion
Theologos
Kinyra
Limenaria
Potos
Astrida
Alyki
Psilli Ammos
PANAGHIA

Besides the town of Kavala and the fascinating surrounding landscape, there are also exceptional islands which attract visitors.

These islands are, however, not only unique for their sun and light. There is also their natural beauty, their lacy coastline with its dazzling white beaches and the blue sea ruffled in summer by the cooling meltemi wind. There are the villages, gazing at the sea from on high, the castles, churches and monasteries.

History and civilization stretch back four to five thousand years here, one must not forget the simple, good-hearted locals who welcome you in their melodious voices.

The islands of Thassos, Limnos and Samothrace are tempting options for those with a desire to explore different and wonderful places, and they have the unique advantage of maintaining a simple, carefree way of life. All three islands are beautiful, each with its own charm and history. Visit them and discover their hidden treasures.

Limnos - Samothrace

Limenas, the capital of Thassos.

Thassos

Thassos is the northern most island in the Aegean, with an area of 379 sq. km., a coastline of 95 km. and a population of 13,000. It lies 19 km from Kavala in Macedonia and only 6.5 km from Keramoti.

Thassos is a large island with lofty pine trees of a special kind with a white and perfectly straight trunk, good for making of ships' masts.

It is a truly beautiful island with a high mountain, Ypsarion or Psarion (1,203 m.), in the middle and a lace-like fringe of beaches wih pure white sand and pine trees, often literally hanging over the sea. the beauty of the spot is frequently complemented by rocks made of white marble.

Thassos has rapidly grown into a large tourist centre. A good paved road rings the island and branches lead into the interior, ending at picturesque villages. This road network is also used by the local buses which connect these villages to the coast and the capital, Limenas or Thassos.

The capital of the island, with 2,400 inhabitants, is bulilt on the site of the ancient town within an idyllivc bay, nestled in the mist of green surroundings.

During the summer, this town, as is natural, garners most of the visitors to the island. the gratest amount of activity is late in the afternoon when the holiday makers take their stroll or sit at little tables on the harbour to enjoy the magnificent sunsets.

1. *The dense woods with the pine trees characterize the island perfectly.*
2. *The shipyard of Limenas.*

3

The archaeological site lies next to the harbour, which in antiquity was used as a naval yard, and is very close to the town's houses. East of this harbour are the ruins of the sanctuary of Poseidon, the sanctuary of Dionysus (both from the 4th century BC) and the Agora.

Further east, on the slope of a pine-covered hill, can be seen the ruins of the theatre (3rd century BC) this theatre, in which performances are still given in summer , underwent alterations at the hands of the Romans. The acropolis commands the summit of the hill. The surviving walls are Medieval and were built on the site of the ancient walls. The descent from the acropolis can be made to the southwest, following the wall.

3. The ancient agora of Limenas.
4. The ruins of the theatre.

4

Night view from Limenaria.

In this case, the visitor will pass succesively through the Gate of Silenus, the Gate of Heracles and Dionysus and finally the Gate of Zeus and Hera. The ruins of the sanctuary of Heracles the island's protector, lie north of the Gate of Heracles and Dionysus.

Near the ancient harbour is the Archaeological Museum with note worthy finds from the island. According to Greek antiquity, Thassus was the son of Poseidon or of King Phoenix, or Agenor and Telephassa. He was the founder and first settler of the island of Thassos, which took his name.

described in one of his poems) was in the end crowned with success and the Parians become the rulers of Thassos. the island began to flourish from that period. A colony was founded on the coast oppossite, the town of Thassos was fortified and developed commercial reletions with Athens, Corinth, the Cyclades and ionia. This prosperity was momentarily interrupted by Persian pillaging which the island suffered twice: in 490 B.C. when Darius tore down the walls of the town and in 480 BC under Xerxes. During the Peloponnesian War the occupation of the

From this island, the first colonists of Kavala, Pangaion and the Thracian coastline set out. Prehistorians believe that, before the Phoenicians came to the island, the first inhabitants were the Kares from Asia Minor and other Thracian tribes such as the Saioi or Edonoi, but that these settlers moved away.

Thassos was already inhabitated at the end of the Neolithic period, most probably by Thracians. At the beginning of the 7th century BC Parians set off on an expedition to conquer the island. Their goal was the mineral wealth of Thassos, specifically the gold and marble. This expedition in which the popular Parian poet, Archilochos, took part (as

island alternated beween Athens and Sparta. In 477 BC it became a part of the Delian league and in 340 BC it was occupied by the king of Macedonian, Philip II. The island flourished under Roman rule in the 2nd and 1st centuries BC. Though the depositts of gold had been excausted, Thassos still had maribe and wine to export. The long Byzantine period followed which was interrupted by the appearance of the Franks and continued for another 50 years there after until the 15th century when the Gattiluci become the rulers of Thassos, staying on the island for about 40 years. the Turkish occupation lasted from 1460 to 1912 when Thassos was liberated and united with Greece.

² The monasteries and churches of Thassos are also spectacular and spring up on every rock and green slope, or on the sea. One of the most beautiful is the monastery of the Archangel with it's marvellous beach. It is a place which emits quietness, peace and security.

There are many tourist resorts on the island of Thassos, which are among the most beautiful in Greece, as well as a large number of other types of accommodation which fill with visitors during the summer and especially around the 15th of August when the island celebrates the Grace of Panagia. The little harbours, ports and bays of Thassos are ideal shelters for private craft, and one of the most favoured excursions is the round of the island, during which one can admire the wild beauties of Thassos.

The picturesque old villages are equally special, perched on the high mountains among the rocks and dense woods, ³ seemingly hiding from watchful eyes. Here time has stopped and the lovable old men in the coffee shops tell tall tales of old events and histories of the island.

The beaches of Thassos are unique jewels of the island, particularly those of Chrissi Ammoudia, Alyki, Paradissos, the beach of Makryammos, Psili Ammos at Poto and the beach at Pefkari.

1. *The ancient acropolis of Thassos.*
2. *The Archangelou monastery.*
3. *The village of Potamia,*
   literally dug into the surrounding green.

1

2

The traditional ouzeries are excellent and offer tsipouro, or ouzo with seafood snacks, and there are marvellous little shops selling souvenirs of the island.

The islanders are widely involved in fishing and the production of olive oil and wine which are famous throughout Greece, as is the honey of Thassos and the authentic little walnut sweets.

Thassos is a wonderful island with thousands of traditions. A small verdant paradise which the people from Kavala visit of every opportunity.

1. The vast beach of Chrissi Ammoudia.
2. The pine trees seem to hang right over the beach of Alyki.
3. The golden beach of Skala Potamia.
4. The beach of Paradissos represents a Heaven on Earth.

4

Kastro and the beaches of Myrina.

Limnos

Limnos has an area of 477 sq. km, a coastline of 259 km, and a population of 16,000. It is 186 nautical miles from Piraeus and its capital is Myrina. This is the island of Hephaestos and belongs to the northeastern Aegean islands. It is located southwest of Samothrace in the shade of the large monastic community of Mount Athos.

In antiquity the island was covered with a thick pall of smoke licked by fiery tongues of flame. These were the fires of its two volcanic mountains. According to tradition, Zeus had hurled Hephaestus into one of them, Moschychlos, to live there outcast from Olympus, the home of the other gods.

The centuris rolled on, the volcanoes grew quiet and as the smoke disappeared an island came into view, which looked like a large open plain. a dry plain with a clayey soil, thirsting for water. Nothing recalled the events of the past.

Only in the west, near Myrina, was there anything strange and it can still be seen.

The enormous black rocks gathered into large piles next to the pure white sand. The steep hills which rise up threateningly above the blue sea. There are tranquil plains linked to the rough mountains. The merry and protected seashore of Myrina mingles with the wild rocks on which the Genoan castle sits. This is what makes Limnos so beautiful and what impresses the visitor.

In addition to Myrina, there are many other small picturesque villages with dentilated coastlines and bays with excellent sandy beaches.

One of the most well known beaches is that of Plati, a busy tourist resort with fish tavernas, hotels and clubs.

When the visitor leaves Limnos, bearing wonderful memories and pictures, he can also take with him some of the famous products of the island, such as cheese, wine and honey.

¹ *Samothrace*

The island of Samothrace is in the north Aegean, north of Imbros, and lies forty kilometres from Alexandroupolis and a hundred kilometres from Kavala. According to mythology, the first settler of Samothrace was Samon son of Zeus and a nymph, or of Hermes and Rhene. The ancient Greeks even believed that the inhabitants of the island sprang up from the soil much earlier than in the rest of Greece. Very famous are the Cabeiric Mysetries that took their name from ² the Cabeiri, who were demons, the children of Hepheastus and Cabiro, daughter of Proteus. The feasts were held at the end of July and it is believed that they still continue at the Christian festival of Agia Paraskevi on the 26th of July which is celebrated by the spring of the plane tree at Palaeopolis. The beauty of the island is unique and wild.

Above all else, there is the imposing mountain of Fengari, the Saos of the ancients, which at 1,611 metres is the highest in the Aegean. Homer mentions that Poseidon sat on its peak to watch the unfolding of the ³ Trojan War, 200 km, away.

From the rocky and sheer peaks of this majestic mountain descend lush green gorges which tumble so steply into the sea that waterfalls are common. sometimes small lakes are formed at the base of these waterfalls. Huge plane trees hang over the lake along with brambles and myrtle.

Samothrace is famed both for its crystal-clear, sparkling clean water and its medicinal springs. The island still lies far from the major tourist activity, despite the enormous archaeological and natural imterest it presents.

1. *Panoramic view of the area.*
2. *The sanctuary of the Cabeiri.*
3. *The waterfalls with their clean waters characterize the island.*

Texts: T. THEODORIDIS, E. KADOGLOU, J. DESYPRIS
Artistic editor: M. TOUBIS S.A.
Photographs: T. THEODORIDIS, D. KOLIOPANOU, A. SAVVOPOULOS,
T. PAPADOPOULOS, Archive M. TOUBIS S.A.

Production - Printing: M. Toubis S.A.